Karate

by Kari Schuetz

BLASTOFF!
READERS
4

BELLWETHER MEDIA • MINNEAPOLIS, MN

Note to Librarians, Teachers, and Parents:

Blastoff! Readers are carefully developed by literacy experts and combine standards-based content with developmentally appropriate text.

Level 1 provides the most support through repetition of high-frequency words, light text, predictable sentence patterns, and strong visual support.

Level 2 offers early readers a bit more challenge through varied simple sentences, increased text load, and less repetition of high-frequency words.

Level 3 advances early-fluent readers toward fluency through increased text and concept load, less reliance on visuals, longer sentences, and more literary language.

Level 4 builds reading stamina by providing more text per page, increased use of punctuation, greater variation in sentence patterns, and increasingly challenging vocabulary.

Level 5 encourages children to move from "learning to read" to "reading to learn" by providing even more text, varied writing styles, and less familiar topics.

Whichever book is right for your reader, Blastoff! Readers are the perfect books to build confidence and encourage a love of reading that will last a lifetime!

This edition first published in 2011 by Bellwether Media, Inc.

No part of this publication may be reproduced in whole or in part without written permission of the publisher. For information regarding permission, write to Bellwether Media, Inc., Attention: Permissions Department, 5357 Penn Avenue South, Minneapolis, MN 55419.

Library of Congress Cataloging-in-Publication Data
Schuetz, Kari.
   Karate / by Kari Schuetz.
      p. cm. — (Blastoff! readers : my first sports)
   Includes bibliographical references and index.
   Summary: "Simple text and full-color photographs introduce beginning readers to the sport of karate. Developed by literacy experts for students in grades two through five"—Provided by publisher.
   ISBN 978-1-60014-570-4 (hardcover : alk. paper)
   1. Karate—Juvenile literature. I. Title.
   GV1114.3.S345 2011
   796.815'3—dc22   2010035458

Printed in the United States of America, North Mankato, MN.
010111   1176

Contents

What Is Karate?   4

Karate Basics   8

The Karate Uniform   14

Karate Competitions   16

Glossary   22

To Learn More   23

Index   24

What Is Karate?

The **martial art** of karate is a sport and a type of **self-defense**. People around the world learn karate to strengthen their bodies and minds.

The word *karate* is Japanese for "empty hand." No knives, swords, or sticks are used in the martial art. Instead, the human body is the weapon.

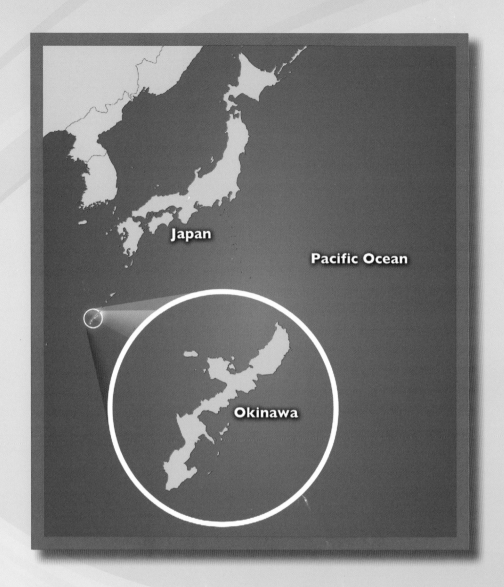

Karate began hundreds of years ago on the Pacific island of Okinawa. The rulers of the island often banned the use of weapons. Okinawans developed ways to defend themselves with their bare hands.

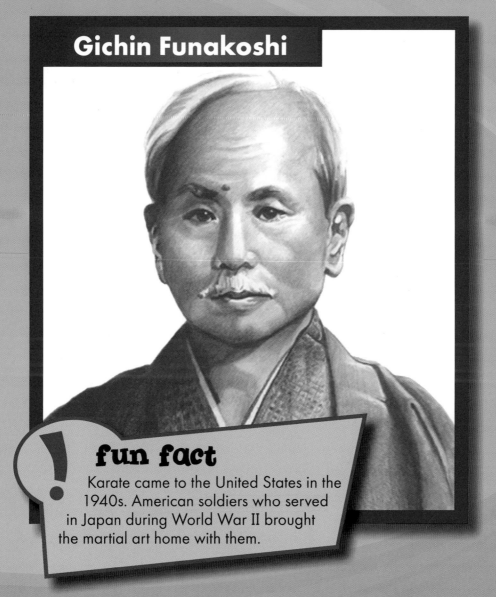

Gichin Funakoshi

fun fact

Karate came to the United States in the 1940s. American soldiers who served in Japan during World War II brought the martial art home with them.

Okinawan Gichin Funakoshi combined the different fighting methods of the island into one style. He brought this style of karate to the Japanese mainland in 1922. People consider him the father of modern karate.

Karate Basics

Over the last century, karate has changed from a form of fighting into a popular sport. Millions of people now attend martial arts schools called **dojos**. They study the sport under masters called **senseis**. People who train in karate are called **karatekas**. Beginners start at the 10th **kyu** and spend years working toward 1st **dan**.

fun fact

Martial arts like karate value respect. Karatekas bow to show respect for their senseis and opponents.

Karatekas learn basic **stances** before they try any moves. These stances help them with their balance and footwork.

The first moves they practice are **blocks**.
It is more important for karatekas to know
how to defend themselves than attack others.

Karatekas then learn attack moves called **strikes**. They learn how to breathe out as they strike. This helps them focus and adds extra power. Some karatekas yell *kiai* to express energy when they strike. Many can kick and punch with enough force to break wooden boards!

The Karate Uniform

A karateka wears a loose uniform called a **gi**. It is usually white and made of cotton. A belt called an **obi** ties around a karateka's waist. The color of this belt depends on rank.

obi

gi ➙

! fun fact

A karateka must perform specific karate moves in front of a sensei to earn an obi.

Obi Colors & Rank
American Shotokan Karate Alliance Ranking Standards

white (10th kyu)

gold (9th kyu)

yellow (8th kyu)

orange (7th kyu)

blue (6th kyu)

green (5th kyu)

purple (4th kyu)

brown (3rd kyu-1st kyu)

black (1st dan-10th dan)

Karatekas practice their moves in bare feet. They wear padded gloves when they try moves against each other, but they stop all strikes before contact.

Karate Competitions

Karate competitions are divided into **kata events** and **kumite matches**. During kata events, competitors perform a series of karate moves on their own or in teams of three.

Several judges score the elements and style of the moves. The person or team with the most points wins. In some contests, judges use flags instead of points to choose a winner.

In a kumite match, two competitors **spar** inside a square with sides that measure 26 feet (8 meters). They earn points for unblocked strikes that land near the head, chest, stomach, and back. The first person to earn a certain number of points wins. The total points needed to win a match varies by organization. If no one earns enough points by the end of a match, the person with the most points is the winner.

fun fact

At many competitions, men's kumite matches last for three minutes and women's end after two minutes.

The best karatekas from around the world compete at the World Karate Championships. The **World Karate Federation (WKF)** holds this tournament every other year.

At these championships, karatekas x-block, roundhouse kick, and karate chop their way to victory. *Kiai!*

fun fact

A karate chop can be used as a strike or a block. The move is also called a knifehand strike because the hand works like a knife!

Glossary

blocks—defensive moves in karate; common blocks are the upward block, downward block, inward block, and x-block.

dan—degree; the highest black belt degree is 10th dan.

dojos—schools where people learn martial arts like karate

gi—the loose uniform a karateka wears; a gi is usually white and made of cotton.

karatekas—people who learn karate from senseis; karatekas train at dojos.

kata events—competitions where karatekas perform a series of karate moves in front of judges; there are both individual and team kata events.

kumite matches—karate fights between two karatekas of the same gender and size

kyu—grade; karatekas begin at 10th kyu and work toward 1st kyu.

martial art—a method of fighting and self-defense; karate is a martial art.

obi—the belt a karateka wears; different obi colors represent different kyus.

self-defense—the act of protecting oneself from harm

senseis—martial arts masters; senseis teach karate to karatekas.

spar—fight; karatekas spar at practice and in competitions.

stances—standing positions in karate; basic stances include the ready stance, forward stance, and horse stance.

strikes—attack moves in karate; kicks and punches are common strikes.

World Karate Federation (WKF)—the official worldwide organization for the sport of karate

To Learn More

AT THE LIBRARY

Buckley, Thomas. *Karate*. Chanhassen, Minn.: Child's World, 2004.

Craats, Rennay. *Karate*. Mankato, Minn.: Weigl Publishers, 2002.

Nevius, Carol. *Karate Hour*. New York, N.Y.: Marshall Cavendish, 2004.

ON THE WEB

Learning more about karate is as easy as 1, 2, 3.

1. Go to www.factsurfer.com.

2. Enter "karate" into the search box.

3. Click the "Surf" button and you will see a list of related Web sites.

With factsurfer.com, finding more information is just a click away.

Index

1922, 7
1940s, 7
blocks, 11
bowing, 9
breathing, 12
dan, 9, 15
dojos, 9
Funakoshi, Gichin, 7
gi, 14
Japan, 6, 7
karatekas, 9, 10, 11, 12, 14, 15, 20, 21
kata events, 16, 17
kiai, 12, 21
kumite matches, 16, 19
kyu, 9
martial art, 5, 7, 9
obi, 14, 15
Okinawa, 6, 7
padded gloves, 15
rank, 14, 15
scoring, 17, 19
self-defense, 5

senseis, 9, 14
sparring, 19
stances, 10
strikes, 12, 15, 19, 21
United States, 7
World Karate Championships, 20, 21
World Karate Federation (WKF), 20
World War II, 7

The images in this book are reproduced through the courtesy of: Lucian Coman, front cover, p. 10; MilousSK, front cover (small); Getty Images, pp. 4-5; Juan Martinez, pp. 6, 7; Dave and Les Jacobs/Getty Images, pp. 8-9; Loretta Hostettler, p. 11; Mike Kemp/Rubberball/Photolibrary, p. 12 (small); Radius Images/Photolibrary, pp. 12-13; Attl Tibor, pp. 14-15; M.E. Mulder, p. 15 (small); Gerard Vandystadt/Tips Italia/Photolibrary, pp. 16-17; Getty Images for DAGOC, pp. 18-19, 21; AFP/Getty Images, p. 20.